L.O.V. E.

Love in front of it

AuthorHouse™
1663 Liberty Drive
Bloomington, IN 47403
www.authorhouse.com
Phone: 833-262-8899

Because of the dynamic nature of the Internet, any web addresses or links contained in this book may have changed since publication and may no longer be valid. The views expressed in this work are solely those of the author and do not necessarily reflect the views of the publisher, and the publisher hereby disclaims any responsibility for them.

This book is printed on acid-free paper.

ISBN: 978-1-6655-1880-2 (sc)
ISBN: 978-1-6655-1881-9 (e)

Print information available on the last page.

Published by AuthorHouse 03/03/2021

authorHOUSE®

* L.O.V.E *

Written By Lashun Mitchell

Story 1

(The Shadow Of Love)

That day I feel in love with that person, boy I could not remember her name. Until 6 months later we had found each other in it was a different filling about been her in a new relationship that had struck my eye knowing that one day we might meet again in I was totally in shock by her new look in personality that made me smile.

By seen her face, in my secrets were out of the box.

Once again, I was trap in this love affair, that was hidden by a married woman that was never caught cheating on her man in for the wrong reason. My doubts were she was back for revenge, to destroy my life but did it really happen to me that day when I was. All alone in my bedroom. In I was awaken by that call, that made me fall in love with that woman, that had stolen my heart. From this terrifying life that I was giving in living in that had put me down in cut from my guilt, in that had made me leave out the door, with nothing to say. But goodbye in I was ashame to admit that she was right, in I was wrong for trying to share my life with her in I was confused about the way that our friendship will turn out difficult, if I was telling the truth from the start.

But maybe if we had more time together, our hopes in dreams could probably came alive, in we both could had made this work out but to me she played the roll as a danger woman, with no feelings it all to step across path in no matter what happens she will always get the last laugh to end your life. In there will be no coming back (from your grave) in also she had some flowers sent to my house unexpected in it made me wonder what is she doing, in what is she trying to prove, that her love for me is stable, in that I had been this fool, for a very long time, but see her mind games, does fool me it all, now that's why I have to leave in go out of town before someone really gets hurt in this shadow of love first I was full of surprises, in second my mind was telling me no, but my heart went alone with it, in see what happen it t??? we both was killed by her ho???

The End

Story 2

(Can We/ Make It Happen)

I woot your love to be all mine in so many words. That no one can come in between us an share our life, while am dying to have you forever and my heart to fill my desire in a perfect combination to hold the key with your soul, that keeps running through my mind, you and I can walk the days of better lasting thoughts, to treat each other in the moment of not being afraid to say I need you with more promises to keep you by my side to built a good strong relationship, with you I surrender different types of emotionally feeling to have you near me understanding how much I feel for your pain that you had been through in the pass but now holding you in my arms in caressing you with ??? feels wonderful, as I whisper and your ear can I have a moment of your time, to open up your heart and give you all of my needs into get closer to you because am fallin so deeply in I want you to be a part of me, with no hesitation just to take our life slow and we will see what will it lead too. By now I just can't let you go without saying. Love is full of surprise and you are the gift, to my love?

The End

Story 3

(What Love Bring's)

One day I feel in love with that person that may me truly happen we was spending time together but all of suddenly her mind begin to wonder else where in I did not notice until I got that phone call from a neighbor down the block, asking me question about Are you in her still dating, because I had seen her with another guy in the last 6 weeks hanging out at his apartment. Playing that loud music, that may me go in knock on the door, in to tell them to quite down, before they wake up the neighbors, in they both told me. We don't have a problem with that, we will turn it down Ok, but as I look and see who it was. My mind was shocked and surprised, that it was her, your girlfriend that you had been dating for about some time now, in so I ask her have she see you, and she said. Who that might be, I don't no you, do you no me, no I don't no you, and so that's why I called you to find out what was going on and ya'll relationship was ya'll splitting up, are was she just having her cake and eating it too, no its not nothing like that I did not no what was going on until you called me OK, so what I am about to do is go over there and have a talk with the both of them and find out what is really going on, with us, because if she has been going over his house every weekend, in supposed to be over her mom's house, that's a very big problem, that me and her both will have to work out without him button and our relation, things might turn out better than it seems to be right now, so may be first I might called her before going over to knock on his door, and something might happen between us maybe we might get into a fight or maybe he might just called the police on me, for knocking on his door while he is having fun with someone else girl friend but (What Love Brings)

Story 4

(My Love)

From the first time in my life. You really attract me, from your everyday sense of humor that had me to smile, and by the look on your face that had me speechless with a strong feeling to ask you out on a date. Once my mind begin to see us coming together my thoughts begin to address your issue with certain decisions to lead us into making it happen with love an promises to arrange my place of heart and your hand to walk down the lane in spread our true love all over the city for what its worth, time will reveal our own secrets for the hold world to no that I love you in yes we will make it happen with love and forever that I need you and want you to be my love always to lean on, and with you as that special love that I can count on.

The End

Story 5

(Guilty)

It was a Friday night in, I was coming from the bar with my co-workers to celebrate my promotion. In it was late in the rain was storming, until I spotted this young lady waiting for her cab, so I approach her. Do you need a ride home, are I can wait with you. Because its kind of dangerous out here. To be waiting all alone by yourself so were is your man it, do he suppose to be picking you up from here, is he running behind, are do you have one it all, that love's to be late all the time, he's probably out fooling around with his secrety, you think so, in she answer, not my man he's faithful. He has a good woman it home, that cooks in clean for him, but why is he always late picking you up is it because his job is on the other side of town, are may be he's out sleeping with the bossess daugther trying to get a raise, but she ends up pregnant, but own the other hand you might be right, his timming has been off, for the last 6 weeks I have been waiting inpatient, for him to speak up. But he does say a word, just how was work today, in what are the kids doing nothing it all, but I have been going through it for some time

The End

Story 6

(Love/ Is Falling Apart)

I never thought that one day our relationship will end this way, because we were meant to be in love. But now it seems that all this time your love wasn't real enough to be with me, your game playing with these other man really hurt me so bad, that I had to leave you all alone and walk away, because you hurt me so bad that I could almost cry, just thinking about our love was growing until you had to cheat on me, with somebody that had went to school with me back in the days, and that made me felt really stupid how you play me that day. See you was supposed to come over, but you went out to the club in had drinks with him, and than later own that night, you went back to his place for a night cap while you was staying at my place, I was so disappointed that I through your clothes out of the house on the front yard so everyone could see how much you mistreated me so badly with no respect it all, you slept around on me with my classmate.

The End

Story 7

(Broken Promise's)

You told me that day when we first met, that our love will not change for the best, but see you lied to see about your promises they were broken, behind my back you cheated on me with that other woman, that I had seen before while we where out shopping last week, I seen how she look at you. But I could tell that ya'll was in love, and all this time you play with for some fool, I though that we where very serious about each other, and it made me and my family both look very stupid with your broken promises, you are a shameful of a man, that told me that very day that we could make something out of ourselves and I beleive you. I must have been blind from your talk in the way you look that had took me to a another level with trust, in your broken promises?

The End

Story 8

(My World Is Your's)

I thought I could trust you but you played me for a fool with your kindness word's, and I fell for it, without thinking first. I though you was the one for me but see I was wrong all this time. My love and trust was set to be with you. For a life time, but all you gave me was guilt, from your behavior that I did not understand. The meaning of your true love, to fulfill my dream and love to go down with lonely teardrop's to bring out the pain that you treated me badley, with no true love it all from your heart and desire one thing lead to another I was blind from your communcation that was eaten inside of my soul that had change ways into leaving you by yourself in this rapture of what you call love. Your mind was self pitty and ful of wicked ways, that I could not control to be with no longer in this relation I had to end it by telling you am sorry about your love, but its not what I need to be love?

Story 9

(About Us)

Should we keep our love together. From the way that you treat me, with no respect it all, now don't you no I was abuse by your love and you driven me insane to beleive that you really love me. But you was playing them mind games all this time, and I was so stupid, that I could even see it with my own eyes, that this so call love was blind from the very first start, and I was looking so foolish for so many years. That my family kept telling me, you need to get out of that relationship and move on but my heart was on a 2 way street trying find love to lean on, but my heart was broken without any feeling to share for the both of us I thought that it was real, all the time that we was together, but I was swallow down a dangerous hole with no way out too find the truth about us.

The End

Story 10

(We Can Do It / Trust Me)

Can we talk about us because I want to love you more, and make you mine forever from the bottom of my heart my feeling's for you is so special, only you can see, that I promise to be there in never leave you alone whatever am going through my mind is only set on your love and that is true. Because nothing can change my life, without having you by my side my love will be and the dark, but since we had been together. My love has been stable and so many way's that no one could change how I feel about you, and from the air I breath our love will last through the days of a life time with no second chances that there will be no other love to walk our way but you are the only one that can satisfied my love no doubt so give it all to me, and let's rest our life together as one

Story 11

(Am Serious)

Am serious about our love in so many ways that every time when I see your face it drives me crazy to not let you go and hold your hand so deeply in my arms. So tight that I can feel your heart pulling on my chest. To relax my mind into saying that I love you forever. And now do you get the point, you mean the world to me, even when am alone by myself. All I do is thinking about you, and what we could be doing today if we was together having a good conversation about us too. Hanging out at my home drinking and eating and watching the best movie on the tube and than later making love to my only girl, that could pleased me in her own ways with careless whisper's that could take away the pain that I had for some manys years.

The End

Story 12

(My Doubt's)

My doubt's about our love could lead me to one thing is to be happy with you and my life, for so many years to come that I pray, that one day my soulmate will appear and my heart standing in my face, saying could I be the one for you, to love you, and that I promise to be your's alway's in forever so please don't go and share my world with me, in we can go many places in talk about us too having it all together. With no else could disturb our talk, as I held out my hand. For your hand to love me inside so deeply, that I will be able to wash away your bad relationship in start on something more beautiful than the shining sun above your life, with some fresh air to make you feel safe and wanted by me your Romeo to grant your wishes and dream's forever, that I will do no doubt.

The End?

Story 13

I did not plan for this to end this way, but our love was so stuck and the mud without a place to go in my life about us. From inside my heart I felt that the time that we were together I must have been a fool to fall in love with you from the start, I was surprise how you look at me. Right in my face in say that you will take care of me, and you promise me that you will never cheat on me, but I must have been stupid to listen to your words and your smile that struck me to be your's, I though you was that perfect one in my world, that had it all for me, but your love push me right in the dark to notice that you was just down right dirty to use me, and walk all over me, with no shame it all, to what you have done, you felt that you was not wrong it all, that I did not see it come, but yes I did.

The End?

Story 14

(Love Again)

So many time's I did not understand for what you was saying to me, but I still love you the way I do, so stop treating me like this, and do me right like you promise to me. Because am still waiting for that moment, to come true, and that special way, so we can walk down that promise land, and I can love you forever and there will be no surprise about how I feel about you with strong feels inside my heart to tell you that I love you. Since the day we mat, you change my life without me knowing it, the pain that I had inside was gone. Forever until you came into my life with that wonderful sense of touch and that smile that took that away from me my pain and ache's was very deeply hurt. By my pass relationship, and now am feeling so better by kindness of emotionally thought's words that struck my mind on the right track to love again?

The End

Story 15

(Love Goe's Up And Down)

You say that our love was meant to be, but all of sudden your love had change for the wrost you begin to play mind game's through this hold relationship, and it did not turn out to be nice, for what you had promise me from the very first start see you brought me gifts and had arranged them dinners for us too eat, and also we had went out for shopping at the finest stores that money could buy, but that one day, that phone call had change my life forever I was introduce to a lady of his, that had stole my heart and took my breath away forever. Like was I drowning in some swimming pool getting deeper and deeper out of the bad relationship, like it was nothing to say are do about the hold love affair that I had gotta myself into that day I was shock about my ???

Chapter 16

(Fall In Love)

All it take's for me is to fall in love with you from the bottom of my heart and treat you so special and never leaving your side, always but are you sure. That you are ready to give us a chance, to say am yours forever in combining our love with promises to fulfill our dreams with no broken feelings that will come in between us down the path to show how much that I care for you always through this life. That we both share this conversation with no hesitation just trust about us catching up with many words to say, but I need you to stay next to me. Because you are everything that I had always wanted in more to lead me through happiness, to forgive my mistakes about the pass, so let's started this future into saying, that you take my breath away, in there is no one like you. That will treat me the way you do

Forever?

The End

Chapter 17

(My Feeling's)

Can we make this love happen please don't break my heart and leave me without nothing to say, but I need you now more than ever. So don't go because am feeling kind of down without you begin next to me we can work thing's out am sorry that I disappoint you can you forgive me, my love please give me another chance, to make you happy again, I did not no what was going on. And what you was going through, but the pain is really hurting me inside. If you walk away from me right now, I promise to stay in not waste your time like I use to. Love you forever in make you mind. By the way, you talk let's start all over again, and keep our life plain and simple to make you mine and I will be your's forever to hold you and my arms in not let you cry a tear, but my feelings needs you. So can we take it slow one day at a time?

The End

Chapter 18

(Forever You)

Since we had been together my love for you has grown much stronger. To take away my pain that I had been gonna through, but now I see you made me fall in love again, and for that reason I promise to share my world with you. Because without you, nobody else could had turn the tables around for me, the way that you did. Now am your's forever. To make that move just you and me will spend time together. In built a very strong relationship in this life our love will be deeper than the sea has you has my soulmate we will last perfect together like no other couple could do the thing's that we do. Can you feel it inside that you are more than enough for me to have. In I can really understand our love will alway's plant its one seed.

The End

Chapter 19

(All/ That I Need)

Now you are all that I need in that I ask for, is to love you by my side, with trust to fill that am wanted. All the time. I can make you be happy, and a new change of life. And to bring you the moment's of a perfect wife, to hold me, and your arm's. With many wishe's to share. Right deep from the heart. My love will travel through your dantasy, and you will be apart of me. With the key to open up, my feeling's to come out specially for you into fill this way again. I have to be serious about you, into make a strong move on you. Everyday I keep thinking to myself is this how love grows, but now I better get myself together, and make your life comfrontable. Just for you will make it happen. Can you see that vision. We will climb the world forever most more than ever with our hand's together you are all that I need?

The End

Chapter 20

(Trust Me)

We was met to be together I no you can feel it inside that my love is place and your heart forever, with the promise's I will keep for sure, to have you understanding the way that I see a future for us. And a hold different life, so will you come with me I will be there for you, to hold your hand, and not let our love fall down with teardrops. But I will try my my best to make you surrounder your feelings again and walk into the open door. For me to love you again, just one more time has I callout your name can't you tell that there is only one thing on my mind is you and that's the truth, when you make that smile on your face I could say, that our day's will change better for the years to come our way with trust has one you're the woman to be. Connect to my soul, with no push away has we talk things over to make it happen?

The End

Chapter 21

(Don't Go)

I though that our love was true until you left me that day it change my hold life. For the feelings I had inside my heart for you, and it had me thinking were did my love go, I though we was met to be but now am lost without your love just trying find my way back to get to your love, and am begging you please, do give us another try because I need you. Has my soulmate will you ever forgive me in be that special one to keep me close in yours arms! And this time I promise, that my love will be better than before, because I was a fool to treat you that way. Am sorry can you think about it, when you are alone at home, thinking about us. In them good things that we use to do together, I no you will miss me because am missing you now and it's written all over my face can't you tell by the way, with my head down and am rockin it side by side, that means that I don't want you to go, and that am sorry?

The End

Chapter 22

(I Can't Live Without You)

A you no I can't live without you because we are perfect together in my heart. My feeling's tell's it all that am the best for you. And can you image me and you making it last forever and this life doing thing's together, like a couple suppose to be, exspressing our feelings and thoughts for each other because no matter what happens, I will still love you alway's, even though if your friends might tell me lie's about you, and try to break us apart, my love for you will keep on going, time after time, even though I haven't seen you and a week, but you said, that we need a little time apart. So you can think to yourself about us. And I can feel that it would work out between us. It might make our love stronger than before! Are you with me because I can't live without you.

The End

Chapter 23

(Time)

The last thing and this world that I don't want to do, is to hurt you, and any kind of way I just want to love you. Like a real man suppose to treat you like a queen, in listen to the feeling's that comes straight from the heart, that you say about us. Has time goes on our love will be so perfect and fine, that your love will be all mine, indeed we will be happy for the thing's that we share and grown together so special, that everyone will notice about our love is so deep because am still in love with you, right at this moment. I could see it and your eye's, that I still have a chance to be and your life, no matter if we don't see each other everyday I could still see you standing next to me, has am whispering and your ear, telling you time will tell about us has the days go by. I will be your forever in my life, to hold our love together?

The End

Chapter 24

(Am Sorry)

I can't understand what happen to our love, was it me that broke us apart. Are was it you that did our relationship like this, but I though that we was really and love all this time begin together, just me and you, and had it all for a very long time, but now it's gone, are maybe we can work it out. And do the right thing. And meet up one day and sit down and talk about us begin back together but I still don't no the reason why were not together. Can you tell me what happen, everyone new that we was and love. Because my feelings for you was so special. And I knew how you felt about me too in your life. Was it my promise's that I couldn't keep. Are you was just tired of our hold relationship movin so fast, but you should've told me, to take it slow, and I would not had fall in love like I did am sorry?

The End

Chapter 26

(Settle-down)

Can me and you see eye to eye if we get a relationship gonna on and we don't have to talk about making love on our first date, just two people having a good conversation about begin together, and taken our time to bond this love with trust, now will that be a problem to workout our chance of begin soulmate's, probably not. I can share my world with you, and satisfied your love forever and to be with you, in will never walk away in leave you lonely with teardrops runninng down your face. I swear to give you all what you need in more, in don't doubt me because I will be that one for you in show you I'm your's. To be deep and love with you, in make you mine, like diamonds is a girl best friends, you will get my love, and see that am serious about you from the begin when we met I knew that our love will be perfect face to face so let's settle down? And give us a try?

The End

Chapter 27

(Stay With Me)

The closest thing to me in life is loving you, and having you as mine to change my life. Do you respect that, together we both will share every moment of happiness. To keep on trying to fulfill our love, into make it better as we relax by the fireplace, while you stay for a while holding hands with me, and having a good conversation about us. Making it happen for the best of us, me and you begin alone together in the same room. So close, throughout the hold relation together giving each other more feeling's of love, with a breeze of touch from the heart inside to fall in love with you. As I whisper please stay the night with me, because I want you to grow on to me, and with me to start our own creation with many word's to stay. Always you will be there truly for me to keep me comfortable every day while we fell each other so come in stay with me?

The End

Chapter 28

(Don't Go My Love)

Sometime's I keep thinking what would I do without you, you brought sunshine into my life in it feel's so good, to have you close to me, and its real love that I never had before. Really the way you make me feel, I can't lie. You got me now so don't go no where, because this is really happen to me, and you're the best, that step into my life. For a very long time, I though I would not ever love again, until I seen you that day smiling at me, and that caught my eye. So deeply that I felt something inside, when you first walk by me I was surprise to notice how you was looking and I was looking like it was love at first site, in you took my breath away from staying, can I talk to you for a moment, and let you no something. You might be the one so don't go no where my love stay awhile?

The End

Chapter 29

(I'm Your's)

Could you be everything to me that I had always wanted and my life. To bring me the love that I need forever by my side into share my heart with. If so am lucky to have you. But can you promise me that you will not leave me, as long as am your soulmate to make you happy and that will keep our love growing perfect, to hold you in my arm's without saying goodbye into kiss your lips, through the night while I make a wish of having you near me into take care of me always into be that one, and only that one that need's you has mine, into fulfill your need's once again. Right now because am trap by your beauty of love and its written all over your face, so please stay awhile, and let me show how I fill because you take my breath away, any given day because I'm yours.

The End

Chapter 30

(Don't Take Your Love From Me)

A love I keep thinking to myself is it you that I need, so don't go away from me. Because you are so special and my life that perfect one, and I will miss you. If you leave me now I might start crying from inside and my feeling's will be torn away without your love. So please stay in let's work it out. Because I need you as my soulmate to bring joy in my life. Everyday I dream of us having what we alway's wanted, and I no that is you, and my world to treat me has the king and you will be mine queen, to fill-up the empty hole, that I was living through, some time with pain on my back, but you took that away. In made me love you alway's like no other could do, take me as yours, and your arms to love you with one more chance in to prove my feeling's still stand.

The End

Chapter 31

(Can We Fall In Love)

Can we fall in love because am all about you, in you will see every word that I say when, I speak of you, without wasting any time from my heart. You can count on me alway's. To chose you and my life forever to be there for you. If any problem's should come across your mind I will be there to handle it for you that very moment with love in understanding to be that man and feel that I'am yours, with no goodbye to say, but to treat you with trust and will never be no fool to disappiont you has long as am close to you in near your soul, to stay without walking away. I just got to say I can't leave you standing in wishe's for one thing, and it might not happen, but am here to spend my thought's, into build my emotion 24/7 on that day when I seen your smile and it took me by surprise, so if I was you can we fall in love?

The End

Chapter 32

(My Thought's Of You)

You are everything to me can't you see. The way I feel about you that I love you and only you and my life you are that special one. That I will keep my promise to take care of. Forever as my soulmate I can't never find another one like you that I admire so deeply. My thought's doesn't change anything from the heart, to show that you are mine every day when we are together you take my breath away closer and closer as we lay I listen to your voice until am a sleepy, dreaming about our love, making us wonder we were friend's before lover's in this relationship I believe and you from the start, and it kept getting better. With so much love to hold on. And make us perfect as one

Chapter 33

(I Feel The Same Way)

And my heart I felt that my search was over. Because I found my love, and it really made me think twice about looking for someone else, because you was standing right in front of me all this long time, showing that you are the one for me, that will treat me right with your trust to be that one for me, as long as am that man. We will be together and forever, and through every moment that we spend our life together. You bring the light into my eye's, and also you brush away the pain that I had when I met you, but now that is over, so now you open up your love. And that is very important to me about how we are going to share our thought's and love in a postive way, to understand that it is good to be real to you. I give you everything and more but do you feel the same way like I do?

The End

Chapter 34

(We Can Do It)

Am slowly fallin for you so what can you say about it all this time. You couldn't tell that my attiuide was steady changing for your love. That I have inside for you, forever has my soulmate I would like for you too be mine, just think for a moment. Me and you can make it happen, like no other couple's can do, we would live through this life that we never had before. A very strong relationship, and our love will be powerful from the heart with open arm's. To fill that I am your man, and that you are my lady, so now am begging you please come and share my world with me and together we will climb the highest mountain and yell out I love you, so do give me a chance, because in time, you will see that, it is always what I wanted and you. Will also see that we will be the perfect one?

The End

Chapter 35

(You Are That One)

So much is gonna on right now, but we don't have to be and love right now. But when it happen we will fall in love at the same time and apart of me, will be a part of you as my soulmate, forever we will be with no problem's on our back's, just love through the day's to come in our life. Will be possible to hold together as one and we will need no other to get us closer. In this moment that we share our feeling's with everything that we got into place our seats as a couple by having a conversation about us planning to do, more for each other, while am hoping that you stay with me, so I can comfronted your love through this wild life that we live, so we can be and peace, in feel the heat raising up above our heads, while we walk in talk, so I can make you mine. From the love that I have inside, to give to you because you are that one?

The End

Chapter 36

(Am Trying)

Can we start all over, and it doesn't have to end this way because your love is so special to me and I need you. To give me one more try, and to make it right. Baby so please understand me. My feeling's from the heart is so deeply in love with you that every time when I closed my eye's. I picture us having a nice quite candle light dinner by the fireplace, trying to make it happen, so let me take you and my arms in squeeze you. From the back of my mind, I was really lonely until I seen you walking bye, that give me a chance to get closer to you once again. I could not stop thinking about the relationship it really hurt me badly, that I ??? that hold right with my face ??? the pillow losing it without you, I just kept on calling you but got no answer and I did not no what was gonna on through your mind could it be someone else, that had stolen you from me?

The End

Chapter 37

(Friends Becomes Lover's)

We don't have to be lonely. But we should be together. And keep our love close. Without begin apart you can alway's count on me to get us through life together as one, into go on and fill your love has need it, and I will treasure your love, like there's no tommorow in to put a smile on your face, forever I can make that promise. Not to let you go and ride away from your love while my heart keeps pounding for you to settle down with me in build a strong relationship for the both of us. To cherish everyday for what is right. To look ahead in our future and have you has my soulmate because, you was bless to come into my life, and stand by me through hard times and good time's but and this life it will be perfect, because I will share it all with you, now do you believe in love J.D that miracle's do work for the best of us to give it a chance in follow our heart?

The End

Chapter 38

(Step Into My Love)

I wanted do it all for you. So will you let me, be that one for you to fall in love with you even though I haven't been knowing you for quite a while I can still be that one, to fit into your life and make things better for the both of us, into lead you through love with a fresh open mind. Into let the pass be gone for us. To start a new change, I want waste your time, but our love will be so special in sweet throughout the day's to come no matter what I say are do, my love will be just for you. And you will fill so relax about having me near you. So I can keep you confrontable, with no hesitation, apart of me, have now reach your heart to see true love, that has arrived in your life and it appear's to be grateful to make you feel good as I look at you once again to step into your love?

The End

Chapter 39

(Let's Give It A Try)

Me and you can make it work no matter if our life ain't the same, we both will feel a different love from the start but than it would change. Us into begin soulmate's, forever my love. Our problem's in pain will disappear and this relationship will standout and a hold different level. With trust and kindness. To fill that our love will go on much deeper every day when I feel your heart against mine, I begin to wonder, yes this is really love by my side, and I don't have to worry about losing you and my life, because you mean something to me, and only I no the love is there in a perfect place as we lay down the truth, to put our love together. Like a puzzle with so many words to say, all together, while were alone I just can't stop loving you in this life, and am not a fool to let you go away?

The End

Chapter 40

(Can We Fall In Love)

Please tell me how can we go about this, our love need's to settle down. And we need's to talk about us. Before our problems get's out of hand and this relationship. Do you no what I mean. Before our love will fall apart, and we both will be lonely staring at the phone. Waiting for someone to call, but our feeling's will be steady slipping away out the door, but am wishin made be I should go by and check up on her to see how she's doing without me, are maybe I should give her a week in than call her to see how she's doing, while am steady pacing the floor. Everyday missing her so much, what do I have to lose. Alot because she is not and my life, I just can't end this. Like this, I love her so much, begin next to me. In my heart feels her everyday present to be mine forever, we have to work something out and stop playing games with each other minds?

The End

Chapter 41

(You Have To Remember Us)

You are the closet one to me and life, that I love so deeply in yes I have been looking, until I spotted your beauty way across the room, and it made you my heart that's why I love you today in without giving you another chance to walk away from me, in leave out the door. Like you did, before we fill in love, it was just to real to see you with someone else. So I had to go for my feeling's in give it a chance to make my life perfect, and there she goe's, a picture of a loving lady that I admire so much that make's me. Call's out her name, when am in the filling of dailing her number. All the time she can't be hurt because my love stands with her through the darkness night while there is a full moon, and she's with me, while am holding her so tight in my arm's so close looking at her smile. On her face knowing that she is one bay chick that am glad to have?

The End

Chapter 42

(Can We Give It/Another Try)

I can't stop loving you, because my life is so lonely without you. So please can we talk about us, because I miss you so much. Everyday, in my mind can't think anymore without you begin by my side. I just sometime's stare out the window waiting on you to come back to me, and I can't sleep at night. Without having them bad dream's when you left out that door that day in you never came back, into my life ever since I have been so unhappy with myself, that I should've probably get on my knees, and tell you that am sorry about everything that I did in the pass, and maybe we can start out the future once again, baby. I do love you from the heart in yes I really do care about you too, but that day it was totally my mistakes the way that I had treated you with no respect it all in am very sorry in foolish about myself OK, now can you forgive me for begin so pitty as a man that suppose to be strong and caring about the one he loves deeply?

The End

Chapter 43

(Our Problem's Are Solve With Love)

You no it don't have to be like this because I feel your pain, and what you are going through, because I have been through the same thing once before and my life with my soulmate, but now we are not together, and I was hurt so bad, like you are OK, but now I have been thinking maybe me and you. Can have a talk about us. Hooking up together, we both know each other pass, and we can see eye to eye on thing's so what is it going to be, lovers are friends. Until we sit down in talk about us making a future out of it, I suppose time will tell about you begin in my life, keeping us together in holding down our love so tight through and thin with no serparation, we can make it work out, on a different level to keep us ahead of everyone else that's watching us. Be together as soulmate now?

The End

Chapter 44

(I Found Love In It Change Me)

I picture you and me loving each other as soulmate's. Because the way I feel about you it bring's sunshine to my heart and when I see your face a smile drive's me crazy to be in love with you, while we are begin scence by our family they no that our love is so deep in special with many more years to come in it's real to hold you. In not dream about you begin here with me, lady you are amazing to have always, that's why I listen to your voice and chose that your love has no problem to go my way, in come down, on my soul, with lot's of vibrations to put me in the moad to love you forever and whisper in your ear to tell you that am so glad that we have each other and so let's make time last until we both are gray in old, my beloved it angel that was brought from heaven to open up my heart for you?

The End

Chapter 45

(Living My Live With You)

Sometime's I feel that our love start long ago. But now it seem's that I was save by your look's and not your heart, but that is not true your love give's me time to surrender my everything. Because you are mine until the end of time, no matter what people say, we rush into this relationship, in did not take our time to catch up on things. But me and you don't have to listen, to everybody talk, just go by our own ways in together we will hold on to our love in a different direction so no one else can lead us. The way that we want it, we will follow what our minds leads to, to get closer to our life as one shaking the hold world, for what we nos what's best for us is more love to handle in hold?

The End

Chapter 46

(Making It Special)

Can we make our love special do you feel what am saying my heart and your's can carry through the darkness of the night with a candle light dinner to surprise the only one and my life that satisfied my heart to be with the one I love forever, you are so important to me I cherish your love from the bottom of my soul that I live through my life, to be with you with no hesisation, to start coming your way with no choice, but to hold you in my arms under the sheet's while I listen to your voice repeating that you love me forever and my life, into show me that our love is focal's only on one thing is begin together

The End

Printed in the United States
by Baker & Taylor Publisher Services